Set Yourself Up to Excel

A Practical Guide to Goals, Habits and Success

Amanda Van Der Heiden

Global Talent Development Solutions LLC
www.GTDScorp.com
contact@gtdscorp.com
ISBN: **979-8-9942006-2-9**

Table of Contents

ACKNOWLEDGEMENTS

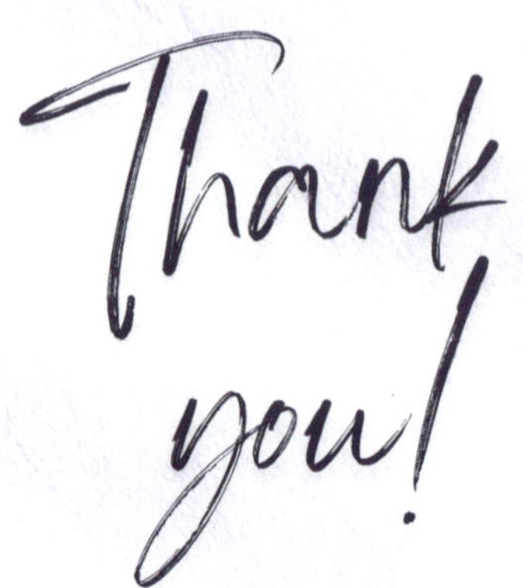

To my children, Zoe and Kai, may you always feel the fear and still take action anyway in pursuit of your goals. I may not always like your behavior, but I always love you. You are becoming the most amazing humans. Keep growing, keep learning and keep trying to be better tomorrow than you were today.

To my parents, who bred me to be a horseback rider. You raised me to be strong, empathetic, dedicated, driven and independent. You showed me the value of hard work and that there is never just one “correct” way to accomplish something. To take in the inputs of others, but decide for myself the path forward. I am grateful for my unique life.

To my family, I’m so lucky to be surrounded by strong, determined women and caring men who challenge norms and always show up when it matters the most.

To my editors, who acted as my sparring partners and thought partners as I refined sections so many times the words had become gobbly-gush to me. Thank you for your insight, enhancement and commitment to making this book the best it can be.

Lisa Christensen
Krzysztof Chorzepa
Donna Horn
Sean DaSilva

To my clients around the world, thank you for trusting me to solve meaningful challenges and for giving me the opportunity to champion change and drive growth.

To my team at GTDS, who continue to raise the bar and share in this journey of lifelong learning and continuous improvement... you are my people!

And finally, a very extra special **THANK YOU** to **Niranjan Dev Singh**. Without your vision, excellence, and commitment, this book would not exist in the form it does today.

Thank you all!

Note from the Author

PARTNERSHIPS THAT EMPOWER,
SOLUTIONS THAT DRIVE IMPACT.

If you are interested in gaining all the benefits of the GTDS Framework for Excellence, check out the full program that builds on these techniques here: https://lms.gtdscorp.com/

I have spent the last two decades focused on how people learn, grow and succeed. I have worked with people from all over the world with diverse backgrounds, experiences and education levels. I have led major Learning and Development initiatives for 40+ Fortune 500 companies in 15+ countries across 12+ industries. I love providing people with the best tips, tools and tricks to help them excel at whatever they strive to achieve.

In this book, you'll discover how to set yourself up for success with tactics you can begin applying immediately. By incorporating these techniques into your daily life you'll find you can achieve more than you ever thought possible. You'll learn how to hack into your psychology, motivation and habits to get real results. You will strategically design a version of yourself who is ready and eager to accomplish your goals.

This dynamic framework includes motivating lessons and actionable exercises throughout the program. This book provides you with the foundational knowledge that will set you up for success in Volume 1 and every volume that follows.

You will secure your journey to success each year by learning how to:

- Lead yourself (Volume 1)
- Influence other people (Volume 2)
- Work with groups (Volume 3)
- Lead through times of change (Volume 4)

The full yearly program provides access to additional self-paced training as well as monthly coaching sessions. Scan the QR code here to explore all the benefits offered by the full program and the physical version of Volume 1.

This book guides you through setting up each component of the GTDS Framework so you can immediately begin designing the life you want with intention.

These valuable tools will teach you to shift your mindset and develop life-altering habits that will lead you to achieve your goals and excel in all you do.

Get ready to learn how you can make the most of every day!

How to Use This Book

This book is designed to be more than something you read, it requires that you **DO.**

Each section introduces a concept followed by actionable exercises to help you apply what you've learned. The goal is continuous improvement over time.

As you move through the book:

1. Take time to reflect before rushing ahead
2. Complete the exercises in order
3. Focus on consistency over intensity
4. Revisit sections as your goals evolve

The GTDS Framework is built on a simple principle:

Small, intentional actions repeated consistently over time create meaningful results.

Get ready to take action, stay consistent and design a life that you are proud of.

Pro Tip: Start Today

Malcolm Gladwell popularized the idea that excellence takes 10,000 hours.

However, most people can become proficient with just 20 hours of intentional practice.

People typically delay starting that first hour for years.

Start your first hour NOW.

SECTION 1

SEE IT. BELIEVE IT. BECOME IT.

The Power of Visualization

VISUALIZATION

What You See Inspires What You Do

In the GTDS Framework, we take the concept of a vision board and include a special insert allowing you to create your own personalized cover. If you do not have access to Volume 1, you may still apply this by creating a paper sized vision board and taping it into your notebook or somewhere that is visible to you on a daily basis.

What you look at every day and what you think about shapes your world. Over time, perception becomes reality. Developing the daily habit of intentionally choosing what you see, focus on and return to will boost your conscious - and subconscious - abilities to move confidently toward your goals.

Physical reminders are powerful tools. Study [1] after study has shown that visual reminders of what matters most to you and what you are trying to achieve can focus your attention, fuel motivation, spark excitement and keep you aligned when life gets busy.

[1]: According to Rogers and Milkman (2016), "Reminders Through Association" (Psychological Science).

It all starts with self-efficacy*, the belief that you can achieve what you set your mind to. Surrounding yourself with tangible reminders of what you want to accomplish activates the part of your brain wired to notice opportunities. When you start noticing opportunities your goal(s) start to feel more achievable. This phenomenon is often called the frequency illusion*, where selective attention* and confirmation bias* work together to train your brain to actively look for ways to make your goal a reality.

Imagine you've made a commitment to wake up two hours early each day to learn a new skill. When the initial excitement wears off, or after a difficult workday, looking at a visual reminder activates your mind and reinforces why all the hard work and challenges are worth your effort. It helps you stay on track when your motivation starts to wane.

Pro Tip: Clear Space = Clear Mind

Your attention is limited and clutter can lead to distraction, fatigue and reduced decision-making ability.

Remove what doesn't matter to focus on what does.

1. Clear your workspace
2. Close unnecessary tabs or apps
3. Only keep visuals that support your goal

When your environment supports your focus, your performance improves.

Change What You See to Change What You Do

Habit research shows that simple environmental design principles can have a major impact on behavior. Put simply, if you adjust your surroundings you can impact your behavior. By keeping only healthy food at home, it becomes more challenging to access unhealthy food. Simply making it more difficult to see and access unhealthy food can help you significantly reduce your consumption. If there are no sweets in the cupboard, you are less likely to eat them because it requires more effort to go out and get them. By adding that little bit of friction it helps you stay on track with your goals.

Another example would be if you wanted to increase your likelihood of exercising in the morning. Create a bedtime habit of placing your exercise clothes and shoes where you will see them when you first wake up. This will encourage you to dress for your morning workout, making it that much easier to get started.

The fun, albeit sometimes challenging, work is thinking of what visual will prompt you to reach your goals.

Actively Visualize Your Goals

Visualization techniques* are used by top performers, athletes and professionals around the world. Neuroscience* confirms that thinking through each step of an activity lights up the same areas of the brain as when you are actually performing the activity. Focusing on visual representations of activities can also evoke similar responses and emotions.

The counter side of this is also true. Fear of a future event can be worse than the event itself. In psychology this is called anticipatory anxiety*, in which the brain cycles through imagined worst-case scenarios or situations, spiking cortisol levels and generating stress, even if nothing bad has happened yet or ever happens for that matter. In simple words, if you think bad thoughts it can have a physical impact on your body.

Your brain is extremely powerful, so develop the habit of focusing your energy on the positive and the goals you wish to accomplish to benefit from these visualization techniques.

VISUALIZE THE POSITIVE

Focus on What You DO Want to Achieve—Not on What You Don't

For example, if your goal is to eat a healthier diet to improve your physical and mental well-being, thinking of a visual that represents your fitness goal will be far more motivating than an image reminding you not to eat your favorite dessert.

Do you see how the picture on the left triggers undesired thoughts of desserts even with a red line through it and the picture on the right leads you to focus on fitness and health?

It's like the commonly used example, "don't think of an elephant." Just reading those words can unconsciously bring the image of an elephant to mind. By working with your unconscious mind's natural tendencies, you'll help train yourself to think in ways that help you and ultimately lead to your success.

SNEAK PEAK

After Developing Your Goals, You'll Personalize Your Visualization Efforts

Before you can begin effectively using personalized visualization techniques, you need to develop and refine the goals you'll be focusing on.

Each of the upcoming sections will lead you on a journey of discovery. You'll learn foundational concepts for exploring, reverse engineering* and developing your goals.

Once you've fine-tuned your goals by completing the book's developmental activities, you'll be ready to begin thoughtfully designing your **Vision Cover*** to remind you why you're pushing yourself to be better. Complete each step in order and enjoy the process of building a solid foundation that will help you achieve your goals. We'll explore how to create your **Vision Cover** in the section **YOUR VISION COVER: Discover How a Vision Cover Can Help You Harness Your Goals** on page 47, where the process is explained in more detail.

Apply your Reading: Visualization

- [ ] Practice visualizing your goals' success each day
- [ ] Write down what you want to be reminded of daily
- [ ] Pick one image that could represent your goal
- [ ] Remove one thing that distracts you

Author Insight

My grandma always said, "If your brain is cluttered, clean your room." Who knew this simple advice was backed by science?!

When I start to feel overwhelmed, I take time to clear the clutter, both physically and mentally. Then, I intentionally focus on what I DO want to achieve and ensure my environment is set up to support me.

It's a simple reset, but it consistently brings me back to clarity, focus and action.

SECTION 2

DEFINE IT. PLAN IT. ACHIEVE IT.

The Power of Goal Development

GOAL DEVELOPMENT

Exploration Leads to Successful Goal Planning

There are countless goal planning templates out there. At this point in your life, you've probably tried a few ways of setting goals. An important element that sets the GTDS Framework apart is a focus on a crucial first step that many people aren't aware of: taking intentional action before setting your goals.

The success of the GTDS Framework centers on intensive personal exploration that will help you understand and develop your goals before you begin planning how to achieve them. The activities and exercises in this book will guide you through the process of confidently defining, then working toward, your goals.

You are probably used to seeing a Goal Planner that looks like this:

GOAL PLANNER

Date :

Main Goal :

Start Date :

Deadline :

List Goal :

-
-
-
-
-
-
-
-
-
-

Motivation :

Reward :

Action Plan :

Review :

Note :

EXERCISE 1

Analyze Why You Want to Achieve Your Goal

Many people think they know what they want to achieve but don't fully understand why they want to achieve it. They jump into finding solutions before they truly understand the problem they are trying to solve, which can lead to unfulfilled goals and wasted effort.

Avoid this common pitfall by developing a clear understanding of the problem you want to solve before you begin planning your goal.

The Five Whys method, popularized by Sakichi Toyoda, Toyota's founder, offers a way to analyze the issue to pressure test your goal. First, you'll write down what you want to achieve and why you want to achieve it. Simply put, you'll examine what you want to gain by achieving this goal.

If you skip this step, you might think you know why you've set a goal, but if you do some digging and ask yourself intentional questions, you may realize this goal is leading you toward a completely different outcome than you intended.

When you put your initial focus on the outcome you truly wish to achieve, you'll be able to find the best way to accomplish it.

For example, if your goal is to lose weight:

1. Ask yourself, "Why do I want to achieve this goal?" and "What will I gain by losing weight?"

   I will feel and look better.

2. Ask yourself, "Why do I want to achieve this goal?" and "What will I gain by feeling and looking better?"

   I will have more confidence and energy.

3. Ask yourself, "Why do I want to achieve this goal?" and "What will I gain by having more confidence and energy?"

   I will go out more and meet people.

4. Ask yourself, "Why do I want to achieve this goal?" and "What will I gain by going out more and meeting people?"

   I will find a significant other.

5. Ask yourself, "Why do I want to achieve this goal?" and "What will I gain by having a significant other?"

   I will be more likely to become a parent.

Note that if any of the above outcome statements were taken in isolation—they would have completely different goals attached to them. By focusing on the fastest path to success to solve your real desire, your action would look drastically different.

Continuing with the above example of a desire to lose weight, the results-oriented action is to exercise and eat a healthy diet to accomplish your goal.

Below you'll see how using the focused questioning technique leads to actionable and achievable goals for each of the five items defined above.

1. **Goal for weight loss:** Exercise five times a week and eat a nutritious diet. (See the Recommended Reading sections for more information.)
2. **Goal for developing confidence and energy:** Complete a weekly micro-challenge* to get out of your comfort zone and build your self-esteem.
3. **Goal for going out more and meeting new people:** Attend one new social or professional event per week and engage in at least one new conversation.
4. **Goal for finding a life partner:** Join a dating site and reach out to one new person each day.
5. **Goal for becoming a parent:** Save up X amount of money by (DATE).

*Micro-challenges are short exercises (or experiments) that encourage consistency and build the habits that will help you reach your goals. They can be created by focusing on one small step you can take each day to move towards a goal. They help you get out of your comfort zone and into your next level.

How to Create a Micro-Challenge

1. **Set your Intention:** Choose one thing that feels slightly uncomfortable or new to you that supports your goal.

    "I will call one person a day"

2. **Make it "micro":** Ensure the task is small enough to be done within minutes or a single, low-stakes situation. Be sure you can easily check YES or NO when asked was this done?

    "Call Amanda today"

3. **Reflect and Celebrate:** Each day, record your event, write how it felt, what you learned and be proud of your action regardless of the outcome.

    "Amanda and I had a great chat. I don't know what I was so afraid of. I am looking forward to calling Zoe next."

4. **Embrace and Create:** Either you succeed or you learn something. Build on this challenge by creating your next one.

    "Now that I have called everyone in my phone, I will expand and talk to one new stranger a day."

The idea behind a micro challenge is to push yourself slightly outside of your comfort zone. By exposing yourself to something new and different just long enough that you realize it wasn't so scary after all and most importantly you *can* do uncomfortable things. You are building your self-efficacy muscle by realizing you can do these things. By doing so you build the momentum to do bigger and better things.

Another common issue with goal setting happens when people take on someone else's goal for themselves. They may wonder why they are unable to get or stay motivated about a goal. If they explore further (through self-guided exercises or with a coach/therapist) they realize the goal wasn't something they wanted to accomplish, it was something other people had told them they *should* accomplish.

For example, deciding to lose weight simply to fit other people's ideal version of you is not a personal goal. In fact, it may be demotivating and ultimately it's mentally unhealthy. Your personal goals are powerful because they are meaningful and motivating to you. If you want to lose weight so that you have more energy and confidence, you become inspired to do the work required to accomplish that goal.

JANUARY

SUN	MON	TUES
4	5 Launch planning	6
11	12	13 Client mtg @ 11
18	19 Gym session	20
25	26	27 Book club

BOOK RECOMMENDA
Power of Habit by Ch

This matters because understanding whether we are intrinsically motivated* (internal fulfillment and purpose) or extrinsically motivated* (external rewards or expectations) helps us align our actions with what will sustain motivation over time. In the above example, seeking someone else's validation is an extrinsic motivator and is a weaker driver during difficult times. Intrinsic motivation, by contrast, comes from wanting to accomplish the goal for ourselves. Make sure your goals are created for you by you. Carefully analyze each goal to find out if it is something you actually want to achieve. If it's not, keep exploring until you find what you really want, then decide on the best way to achieve it.

Once you know WHAT you want to achieve and you feel confident about WHY you are achieving it, the fun begins! This is when you start intentionally designing your roadmap to success. This book provides easy-to-follow steps that will lead you through this life-changing process.

EXERCISE 2

Reverse Engineer Your Goals

At GTDS, we guide people to achieve meaningful success through strategic design. Instead of starting tasks and hoping they lead to results, our system will help you begin with the desired outcome and **reverse engineer*** the actions needed to achieve it. This approach allows you to move smoothly from big-picture vision to clear, simple, daily actions.

Rather than creating goals that feel overwhelming or vague, you'll break them down into specific, measurable snapshot moments—actions you can confidently answer with a YES or NO when asked, "Did you accomplish this goal by (DATE)?" Think through your personal and professional goals, then work backwards using the structure on the next page.

Here's an example of how to break down a goal and answer key questions about it:

Annual	What is your number 1 priority for this year?	Get a new job
Quarter	What 4 milestones will add up to a win?	Complete at least 3 interviews per quarter
Month	What 12 meaningful steps will move you forward?	Apply to 10 jobs every month
Week	What 52 actions will keep you on track?	Reach out to 3 unique people in my network every week
Day	What is the 1 thing you will do daily to support this goal?	Review job postings daily
Task	What item(s) or actions are required to complete the goal?	Today I will update my resume and LinkedIn profile

Each level, starting from annual and working down to task, should feel increasingly clear and actionable.

By **reverse engineering your goals**, you transform intention into execution. Big goals feel achievable because you always know exactly what to focus on next and you have broken it down into manageable, actionable steps.

Progress happens one clear action at a time.

Prioritization Leads to Realization of Your Goals

While the first step in this exercise is brainstorming all the options, the next critical step is prioritizing the actions that will lead to the biggest impact and placing them in the order of importance.

The action at each level should be run through the following pressure test:

1. Why do I need to complete this action?
    - Example: "Why do I need to complete at least three interviews each quarter?"
        - "Because with each interview I complete, I gain the practice required to succeed."
2. How does this action help accomplish my #1 priority?
    - Example, "How does completing at least three interviews each quarter help me find a new job?"
        - "Interviews are a necessary step in finding a new job and it is a numbers game. The more I do, the more likely I will be able to secure a new job."

3. Am I completing actions in the order that will result in the biggest impact?
   a. Arrange each action in the order that will drive the biggest impact to smallest impact.
      - Example: "Am I completing at least three interviews at the correct stage of the process?" *"Yes, by updating my LinkedIn profile first, then reaching out to at least three people in my network weekly, then researching job postings, and applying to jobs consistently, I will be able to secure at least three interviews quarterly.*

Here is why the above actions were put in that order: Updating your LinkedIn profile and resume allows hiring managers to find you and prepares you to apply to jobs.

Reaching out to people you know is a critical next step, as sharing that you are seeking your next opportunity significantly increases your chances of success. Research indicates that 70–80% of jobs are secured through networking instead of public postings. Because of this, building personal connections becomes one of the most powerful strategies for finding your next role.

Did you know that your network extends beyond your immediate contacts? One of the most underutilized opportunities comes from weak ties* (acquaintances or friends of friends) who often provide access to new information and opportunities outside your usual circle.

Next, move to job postings—this is where organizations are actively signaling that they are hiring. A quick warning, not all postings represent immediate or active opportunities. Some roles may already be filled, paused or used to build a pipeline of candidates. This is why relying solely on job boards can be limiting. For someone who has been on the job hunt before, you know how emotionally exhausting it can be. Keep pushing forward, taking action and I know you will succeed!

To increase your chances of success, combine job applications with networking and direct outreach. When possible, connect with someone at the organization to gain insight or visibility beyond the posting.

Here's why interviews come last: while they are the most critical step in securing a new job, you won't get the opportunity without first completing the steps that lead to them.

Next you'll need to select the top three action items that will make the biggest impact. By focusing your energy on these key action items, you'll prevent overwhelm and improve your success rate.

Now that you know which actions will yield the best results, add them to your calendar. Time blocking* ensures you're scheduled to make progress.

Pro Tip: I like to guarantee my progress by blocking time in my calendar and by reviewing my current priorities on a regular cadence.

For example, you might say, "I want to learn a new language," but if you don't have time scheduled each day to work on it the likelihood you'll achieve your goal is significantly lower than if you were intentionally blocking time each day and tracking your efforts.

Breaking accomplishments down into their smaller essential parts can be very powerful. It will help you become hyper-focused on the items that will lead to the greatest success.

Don't Just Act SMART, Act SMARTER

While it might seem simplistic, there are a few critical reminders you should review before writing down your goals.

You may have heard of SMART goals, but here at GTDS we develop SMARTER goals*.

Specific: Can someone else understand what you're trying to achieve without any explanation?

Measurable: Can you easily answer with a YES or NO that your goal has been completed?

Achievable: Can you realistically reach your goal in the timeline you have set?

Relevant/realistic: Will achieving this goal serve your overall mission?

Timely: What is the deadline for your goal?

Evaluate: Did you accomplish your goal?

Refine: Is something not working? Readjust and create an updated plan based on your evaluation.

Now that you've seen how to make SMART goals even SMARTER through evaluation and reassessment, you're ready to move forward.

Now use what you learned through **reverse engineering your goals**, prioritizing the order of importance and ensuring your goals are SMARTER to fill out your plan for the next month.

WHAT DO YOU WANT TO ACCOMPLISH?

ANNUAL GOAL: ____________________

	WEEKLY GOAL	TASKS
JAN Goal	1 ____________ →	• ______ • ______
	2 ____________ →	• ______ • ______
	3 ____________ →	• ______ • ______
	4 ____________ →	• ______ • ______
	5 ____________ →	• ______ • ______
FEB Goal	1 ____________ →	• ______ • ______
	2 ____________ →	• ______ • ______
	3 ____________ →	• ______ • ______
	4 ____________ →	• ______ • ______
	5 ____________ →	• ______ • ______
MAR Goal	1 ____________ →	• ______ • ______
	2 ____________ →	• ______ • ______
	3 ____________ →	• ______ • ______
	4 ____________ →	• ______ • ______
	5 ____________ →	• ______ • ______

Be Prepared for Anything and Everything

Another vital step is to create contingency plans*.

Remember the earlier section that encouraged a focus on the positive (exercising and eating a healthy diet) instead of on the negative (not eating your favorite desserts)? Well, there are exceptions to most rules and this is one of those exceptions. You need to think about what challenges you may encounter to ensure your success. Here's how that works in action. Spend time thinking about anything and everything that could get in your way. As you work towards your goal, what obstacle might get in your way and impede your progress? Then create a plan to overcome each of these potential roadblocks.

Your contingency plans don't need to be overly complicated, you can simply write out a series of if/then statements on a piece of paper, on your phone, or in a document. Below you can see just how easy this process can be.

Goal: I plan to take a one-mile outdoor walk every morning.

Contingency Plans:

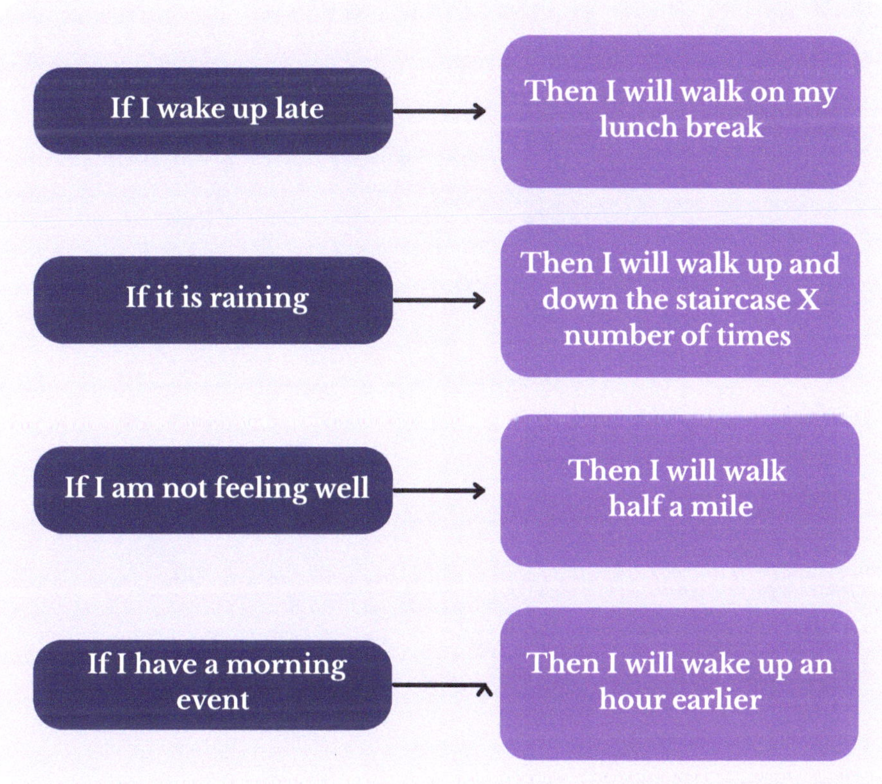

The more potential problems you can find a solution to in advance, the less likely the unexpected will be able to derail you in the moment.

Get Ready, Get Set, GO!

Once you have clarified your priority, set your intention and are confident you are working to solve the correct problem, it is time to START!

Getting started is the most important step to actually achieving your goal. So many people get stuck in analysis paralysis* or in learning, reading or researching that they never begin working toward their goal.

Pro Tip: Start with the smallest possible step forward. You have to break your goal down into the smallest possible steps to ensure you know where to start, how to build momentum and gain the confidence that will lead you to where you want to go.

Be Consistent and Rely on Measurement

Once you take the first small step, recording and measuring your actions is essential. Your behavior and actions are in your control, while the outcomes may not be. Consistency is key and will build your path to success. By measuring the effort you put in, you can see trends, make adjustments and keep your motivation high as you continue to make progress.

Analyzing your efforts is key to reaching success. The first step is gathering data and metrics, then reviewing them regularly. Analyze trends and create reflection points to move confidently toward the results you want.

Pro Tip: When I get ready to make long-term behavioral changes, I always make sure I verbally tie my new goals and actions to my new and improved identity. This may sound simple and silly, but it is a powerful tool.

As humans we want to align our actions to the beliefs we hold about ourselves, but when the two are not aligned it creates discomfort called Cognitive Dissonance*. You can use this to your advantage by creating a foundational belief and letting your subconscious align your actions accordingly. As it applies to working toward your goals, once you believe something to be true to preserve your mental self-image your actions must match.

For example, if you redefine yourself as a healthy person then eating junk food every day will create discomfort because it is not aligned with your new image. People unthinkingly jump through mental hoops to align how they describe themselves with how they act each day.

Look closely at what you think versus what you do, then work to make the changes needed to ensure that your internal view and external actions are consistent. Reinforce your goals by verbally confirming your commitment to consistency, "I am a healthy person, so I eat healthy foods."

Tying your goals to your identity increases your intrinsic motivation to keep going when things get difficult. You'll be motivated by the act itself instead of the external reward or outcome.

This is critical because as mentioned earlier you can put in a lot of effort and if you don't see immediate results you may get discouraged. This is why focusing on your actions and what you **can** control will keep you motivated when the results take a little longer to achieve than what you had hoped for.

One of my favorite analogies references an ice cube in a 25°F room. If you begin raising the temperature one degree at a time you will not see a change in the ice cube until you reach 32 degrees. So, if your focus is on the ice cube at 25, 26, 27, 28 degrees...you will not see a change. It will seem like nothing is happening. But if you focus on the thermometer, you can clearly see that your efforts to increase the room temperature are working. This is the key: make sure your focus is on the correct measurement even if your ultimate goal is to melt the ice cube.

NOTES

Develop a Note-taking Habit* to Keep Yourself on Track

The full GTDS Framework's workbook includes blank pages for recording notes throughout. Write down favorite quotes that inspire, fuel and excite you. Include mantras and sayings that empower you to greatness. Write down new concepts or words that you want to remember.

Note-taking is an additional tool to help you capture your insights, reinforce what you are learning and stay aligned with your goals.

You are on a journey to become a better you. By recording this process, over time this becomes your personal playbook*—a collection of thoughts, insights and reminders you can return to when you need clarity, direction or motivation. They help remind you of the moments that stand out. On days when you feel stuck, unmotivated, or uncertain, revisit your notes. They will help you reconnect with your purpose and re-energize your next step forward.

How to Use This Section Intentionally

Take your note habit to the next level by adding purpose:

- Capture one key takeaway from anything you read, hear or experience
- Write down what it means to you
- Identify how you will apply it

Simple Note Framework (Use Daily or Weekly)

Here are a few additional ideas you can log

- Insight: What stood out to me?
- Meaning: Why does this matter?
- Action: What will I do with this?

Exercises to Build the Habit

1. Daily Insight (1 Minute)

Write down one idea, quote or lesson from your day. What is one thing you want to remember from today?

2. Weekly Reflection Note

At the end of the week, review your notes and capture:

- One pattern you noticed
- One idea worth applying
- One action to take next week

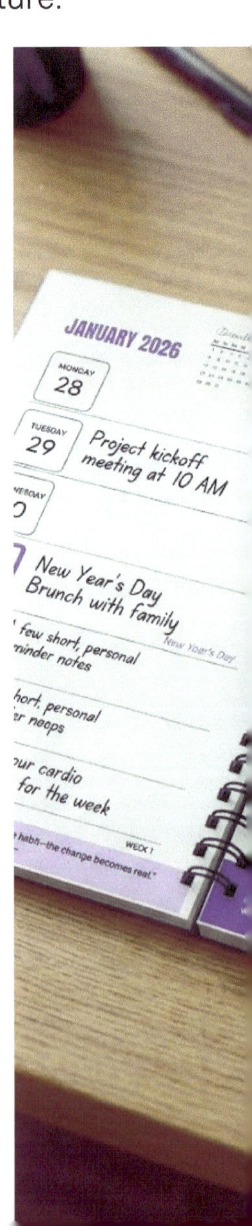

3. Build Your Personal Playbook

Create sections within your notes such as:

- Quotes that motivate you
- Lessons you have learned
- Reminders you need often
- Ideas you want to explore

4. Revisit & Reinforce

Once a month, review your notes and highlight:

- What still resonates
- What have you applied and with what success
- What you want to focus on next

Pro Tip: A single meaningful note each day compounds into clarity, confidence and growth over time. Have I mentioned consistency is key?!

When You Feel Stuck, Do This

Even with the best plan, there will be moments when you feel stuck, unsure or unmotivated. That is completely normal AND you should still take action anyway.

Use the 3-Step Reset

When you feel stuck, ask yourself:

1. **What is the next smallest step I can take?**
   Make it so simple it's impossible to avoid.

2. **What is in my control right now?**
   Focus only on actions.

3. **What would the best version of me do next?**
   Act from identity, not emotion.

Pro Tip: Remove friction and create motion.

- Make it easier to start
- Lower your expectations
- Focus on progress and build from there
- Momentum creates motivation.

One Action. Right Now.

Write down the next step you will take

Apply your Reading: Goal Development

- [ ] Run your goal through the 5 Why test
- [ ] Select the goal and reverse engineer the action
- [ ] Block time in your calendar to accomplish your goal
- [ ] Write your goal using the SMARTER framework
- [ ] Create at least 3 if/then contingency plans to support your goal

Author Insight

I've always believed that where there is a will, there is a way. As I've learned more about goal setting and achieving results, I've come to realize it's also a numbers game, an input/output equation. The more strategic you are in defining the right goal, the clearer and faster your path to success becomes.

In 2018, I was laid off and quickly secured a contract role with a defined end date. When that ended in 2019, I found myself interviewing for both full-time and contract positions across People/Program/Project Management, Change Management and Learning & Development. I tracked everything in a spreadsheet, but because I wasn't fully clear on what I truly wanted, it showed and it took longer than expected to find a job.

Once I clarified my goal and aligned my actions, everything accelerated.

SECTION 3

OWN IT. ALIGN IT. BUILD IT.

The Power of Intentional Design

SELF-CARE LIST

Take Care of Yourself to Take Charge of Your Goals

The GTDS Framework is all about designing individual days that lead to the biggest overall impact.

Life gets busy. When schedules fill up, it's easy to move through your day, week or even month without intentionally checking in with yourself. The **Self-Care*** list is designed to help you pause, reflect and stay aligned with the habits that support your overall well-being.

Everyone's self-care needs are unique and they can shift from year to year. This worksheet is designed to help you identify the top ten activities that will make you healthier, happier and more balanced.

It's important to remember that these activities can include small habits or larger commitments, but the key is consistency! Developing these daily habits will have a big impact over time.

A few important guidelines:

- **Set your Self-Care List for the entire year:** Instead of changing your list monthly or quarterly, take the time to reflect on what truly matters to you this year and establish a consistent self-care routine. This will give you a clearer snapshot of your growth over the course of the year.
- **Focus on core areas:** While your list can include a wide range of activities, the GTDS Framework recommends including at least one activity from each of the following categories:
  - **Rest:** Prioritize quality sleep for energy and mental clarity. Each person has unique sleep needs, but general guidelines for adults recommend between seven to nine hours of sleep.
  - **Diet:** Consume nutritious foods that promote your health
  - **Physical Activity:** Stay active; regular movement keeps your body strong and your mind clear.
  - **Mental Care:** Use practices that help maintain psychological well-being like mindfulness exercises
  - **Personal Relationships:** Spend time nurturing meaningful connections.
  - **Self-Development:** Engage in activities that promote personal growth.
  - **Something Exciting:** Find activities that make you eager to start each day.
  - **Non-Negotiables:** Commit to activities you don't enjoy doing, like taking vitamins or using lotion, but know are essential for your health.

By keeping your list consistent and tracking your progress, you'll create a clear and actionable guide to maintaining balance and wellness throughout the year.

It's simple: Create awareness. Track consistency. See progress.

Physical Self-Care

	Y	N
Slept at least 7 hours	◯	◯
Ate Whole30*	◯	◯
Exercized OR 10,000 steps	◯	◯
Drank 8 glasses of water	◯	◯
Took vitamins	◯	◯

Mental Self-Care

	Y	N
Meditated	◯	◯
Read	◯	◯
Recorded a gratitude	◯	◯
Reflected in a journal	◯	◯
Stayed within my screen time boundary	◯	◯

Social Self-Care

	Y	N
Intentionally connected with others	◯	◯
Spoke to a friend or family member	◯	◯

Spiritual Self-Care

	Y	N
Volunteered or contributed to something bigger than myself	◯	◯
Maintained a healthy balance between alone time and connection	◯	◯

An example may be:

	M	T	W	TH	F	SA	SU
Slept at least 7 hours	☑	☐	☐	☑	☐	☐	☑

Design your own list to intentionally put time toward what matters most.

Be sure each item is *Specific, Measurable, Achievable, Relevant and Timely.

	M	T	W	TH	F	SA	SU	2026
1. ______________	☐	☐	☐	☐	☐	☐	☐	☐
2. ______________	☐	☐	☐	☐	☐	☐	☐	☐
3. ______________	☐	☐	☐	☐	☐	☐	☐	☐
4. ______________	☐	☐	☐	☐	☐	☐	☐	☐
5. ______________	☐	☐	☐	☐	☐	☐	☐	☐
6. ______________	☐	☐	☐	☐	☐	☐	☐	☐
7. ______________	☐	☐	☐	☐	☐	☐	☐	☐
8. ______________	☐	☐	☐	☐	☐	☐	☐	☐
9. ______________	☐	☐	☐	☐	☐	☐	☐	☐
10. ______________	☐	☐	☐	☐	☐	☐	☐	☐

Once you have created your list and set targets for the year, **reverse engineer your goals** to ensure your success. While the goal is to do each of your **self-care** activities daily, remember that it might not always be possible.

Pro Tip: I like to review my scores for each week, month, quarter and year. This habit provides me with valuable insights into my overall well-being and progress. It also helps me course correct if I need to restructure my days to complete my items.

Mark your **self-care** activities daily and score them weekly. When you have your numbers for the month, try to beat those numbers during the upcoming month. Gamifying* your experience can keep it fun and make it extra rewarding.

When I first began this exercise years ago the Self-Care items used to change frequently. After years of doing this exercise, my self-care routine has mostly stabilized. I know the key areas I need to focus on daily to set myself up for success. Now I up the ante each year by increasing the number, complexity or level of each activity.

For example, I have a Self-Care category focused on learning and reading. A few years ago, my Learn/Read goal was simply to read for ten minutes a day. Watch how it progressed over the past couple of years.

Pro Tip: I've been using this framework for years and I love seeing continuous improvement.

Year	Amount of reading time in minutes	Days Completed
2024	10	270
2025	15	290

For 2026, I've expanded the goal to read for at least thirty minutes a day and complete this 300+ days this year. See how I'm building the habit and increasing the output over time? The category stays the same, but the stakes are higher.

Using this example, here's how to **reverse engineer** a goal down into achievable individual days:

Learn/Read goal: 300 days in 2026
Each month I will need to read at least 25 days
(300 days/12 months=25 days a month)

Each week I will need to read approximately 6 days
(300 days/52 weeks=6 days a week)

As you move forward with the GTDS Framework for Excellence over the years to come, striving to beat your previous years' numbers will help you stay motivated and have fun. It will ensure you are a better you than you were last year.

Design Your Ideal Day

Before you define your year, start with your day.

Your life is built one day at a time.

If you could design your ideal day, what would it look like? Think of a realistic, intentional day that moves you forward toward your goals.

Morning
How do you want to start your day?

Work / Focus Time
What are your top priorities and what do you enjoy doing the most?

Energy levels
What brings you the most energy and what habit do you have in place to support that?

People & Connection
Who do you want to connect with?

Evening
How do you want to end your day?

Reflection
What is one action or change you can make tomorrow to better align with your ideal day?

Win your day and you win your year!

WORD OR THEME OF THE YEAR

Use the Written Word as a Compass to Guide You

How do you prioritize your time and ensure that your effort is translating into real progress, not just busy work? Choosing a cornerstone **word or annual theme** helps guide your decisions, focus your energy and align your actions on what truly matters.

Your Word or Theme of the Year* acts as a filter. When faced with decisions, distractions or opportunities, you can ask: Does this align with my word or theme? If the answer is yes, it belongs. If not, it may be time to pause or recalibrate.

Choose a word or theme that feels meaningful, energizing and powerful; a word or theme that works for you and supports the direction you want your year to take.

Choosing your **Word or Theme** of the Year may seem simple, but it should resonate across all areas of your life. This is a word or theme that empowers you and fuels your drive for the year ahead. It's deeply personal and subjective. What it means to you may be entirely different from what it means to someone else.

The right word or theme should give you clarity and motivation, especially during moments of doubt or indecision. When you're unsure about the next step, this word or theme should serve as your anchor, reminding you of your true priorities and **YOUR VISION** for the year

Take Time to Choose the Best Word or Theme to Guide Your Year

This is not a five-minute task. Spend time reflecting, experimenting with different words and exploring synonyms through resources like search engines, dictionaries or a thesaurus. Your **word or theme** should become the cornerstone for your year. Something that inspires you to move forward and helps you align your actions with your bigger goals.

When you review your goals for the year, think about which word or theme will keep you focused and driven. Let it be the guiding light that helps you achieve your vision for the year ahead.

Bring Your Word to Life

Your Word of the Year is more than a word, it will be your rock that guides you this year. Leverage its power by bringing it to life through your actions.

Ask yourself:

- What does this word look like in action?
- How does this word show up in my daily habits?
- What choices would align with this word?
- What will this word repel?

Use these questions to guide you into the next step.

YOUR VISION COVER

Discover How a Vision Cover Can Help You Harness Your Goals

The GTDS Framework puts a new spin on the concept of a vision board, inviting you to use the knowledge you'll gain in this book to create a personalized **Vision Cover** that inspires you to achieve your goals.

Once you've completed all the foundational exercises leading to this point, you'll be ready to design your Vision Cover.

A Vision Cover is a collage that represents the person you want to be this year, the goals you wish to achieve and the results you plan to gain.

Volume 1 features a special insert made to display your Vision Cover. (If you're reading the ebook or listening to the audiobook, you'll still create a Vision Cover that will provide you with daily encouragement. Instead of using Volume 1's insert, you'll display it in a location that's a key part of your daily routine such as the cover of a notebook, your bulletin board or your mirror.)

Reflect and Brainstorm Before You Put Your Creativity to Work

You can add anything to your **Vision Cover**—photos, text, illustrations—but whatever you choose, make sure you select visuals that connect with your **Goals, What you want to accomplish, Self-Care List** and **Word of the Year** in ways that will empower you.

Your inspirations may reach back to your childhood or they may be more recent.

When you think of achieving your goals:

- Do you think of specific people? Family or friends? Athletic figures? Scientists? Authors? Musicians? Successful businesspeople? Historical figures?
- Do you think of words? Quotations? Song lyrics? Poetry? Powerful words?
- Do you think of images? Fitness? Sports? Nature? Cities? Beautiful homes? Impressive offices? Animals? Team logos? Corporate slogans?

These are a few examples to get you thinking. Whatever inspires you, you can include on your Vision Cover!

Apply your Reading: Intentional Design

- [ ] Review your goals from the previous section
- [ ] Create your **Self-Care List**
- [ ] Select your **Word or Theme of the Year**
- [ ] Build your **Vision Cover**
- [ ] Place it somewhere you will see it daily.

Author Insight

I've been developing and refining this system for over a decade. Each year, I continue to evolve it by adding and adjusting activities to enhance its overall effectiveness.

When I first started, some of these exercises felt obvious or even a bit silly. But through consistent application over time, I've experienced just how powerful they can be. The value in these exercises is in returning to them, refining them and allowing them to shape your thinking and actions year after year.

On the following pages, I'll walk you through how I built my **Vision Cover** for the year to help bring this process to life.

VISION COVER EXAMPLE

This is a personal example– It is NOT a Template

As you get ready to create a **Vision Cover** that will motivate you in your own special way, I'd like to share my Vision Cover and the story behind it, to help you get started. I will deconstruct certain aspects so you can see my thought process as I created my Vision Cover.

Remember: Your Vision Cover will be completely unique... designed for you by YOU.

This following example is solely to encourage you to think about your own life experiences, personal inspirations and goals you want to achieve.

A Lifelong Ride Toward New Goals

Here is what you need to know about me. I am a horseback rider. My parents met through their individual passions for horses and have spent their entire lives in various aspects of the horse world.

My mom was obsessed with horses and left her entire world behind to work 12+ hours a day riding, coaching and teaching horseback riding while managing other people's farms. She teaches horse science and management for specialized vocational schools for high school students, runs college programs and runs camps. She competes in 3-day Eventing (even at 70 years old!) This is one of my favorite pictures of her - jumping over a picnic table while pregnant with me! I am inspired by my mom's singular determination and fearlessness and have learned what it truly means to push through pain, fear, shortcomings and "do it anyway" mentality.

My dad was born in the Netherlands and at just 16 years old left his home to work with horses. He came to the U.S. when he was only 18 years old and worked extremely hard taking care of other people's horses and farms. His focus was on the racetrack and eventually breeding and raising young horses to reach their full potential. He rode and trained horses and competed in show jumping. Here is one of my favorite pictures of my father who has always inspired me by how he meets people and horses, where they are and guides them to their full potential through support, encouragement and challenge. It is a special skill to set people up for success.

As you may have guessed by now, my parents met through horses and I was raised in the horse world. It taught me work ethic, determination, grit, empathy and so much more. I remain grateful for my childhood and try to pass on the value to my own children.

Each of the photos on my **Vision Cover** remind me how I've developed over the decades.

This was me at about 2 years old, when I won my first place ribbon.

This was me at 12 years old, doing something out of my comfort zone. While my mom likes the thrill of eventing, I prefer riding in a ring with jumps that have the ability to fall down.

When I look at this picture I can still feel it. It takes me back to the emotions a few moments before the jump when I was afraid, but I pushed myself through and felt so proud after I had accomplished jumping over this out-of-the-ring, if-you-mess-up-you-die jump.

By the time I was 22, my hard-won skills and confidence allowed me to take this young horse through his first major jump to see his full potential.

When I look at both of the horse jumping photos they still energize and inspire me in very different ways.

After 32 I welcomed the next generation of riders with my own children. Here is a picture of my daughter at about 2 months old and my son at his 2nd birthday party.

My **Vision Cover** energizes and serves as a powerful reminder that being brave means being afraid and doing it anyway. Each of the horse photos are also hung on the walls of my home and office as constant reminders of the gains I've made by pushing through my fears.

Think about the photos and art you display in your home or office. Why did you select them? How do they make you feel? What are they inspiring you to do? After you've spent some time brainstorming, you'll be ready to get creative!

In addition to horses, I am a lifelong learner and believe strongly in helping other people achieve their goals. To accomplish this I need to continue to learn and grow myself in order to help other's be better. Each year I strive to acquire new skill sets through certifications, workshops and books. On my vision cover I include these to challenge myself.

My company, Global Talent Development Solutions (GTDS), is a learning and development company dedicated to helping individuals, teams and organizations excel - especially during times of change. We partner with organizations to ensure they have the right people, processes, tools and training to succeed. From learning strategy and implementation to program management and evaluation, we deliver end-to-end solutions that drive real impact. Through our global network of expert consultants, facilitators, instructional designers, developers, coaches and AI specialists, we bring the best talent to every engagement.

My work fuels me as I love helping other people so it is a key component of my **vision cover**.

So now I will put it all together for a visually appealing and energizing **Vision Cover**.

SECTION 4

RECORD IT. REVIEW IT. REFINE IT.

The Power of Planning

Journal and Log Your Way to Success

Journaling and logging have so many benefits. The GTDS Framework provides many opportunities to journal and reflect that build on themselves and will help you throughout each section.

Planners, Calendars, Worksheets and More

Quarter Planner

Use your Quarter Planner in a way that best supports your goals and personal system. Here are just a few ways that GTDS graduates have successfully utilized these pages:

1. **Highlight Special Days:** Mark key dates, milestones or events that are significant to your goals or personal life.
2. **Track Self-Care Wins:** Highlight the days when you achieve a perfect score on your **Self-Care** Worksheet as a reminder of your progress.
3. **Create Your Own System:** Customize the planner to fit your needs. Whether it's tracking specific habits, setting mini-goals or organizing your time.

2026 QUARTER 1 PLANNER

JANUARY		FEBRUARY		MARCH
THU	1	SUN	1	SUN
FRI	2	MON	2	MON
SAT	3	TUE	3	TUE
SUN	4	WED	4	WED
MON	5	THU	5	THU
TUE	6	FRI	6	FRI

2026 QUARTER 1 PLANNER

JANUARY

1	THU	
2	FRI	
3	SAT	
4	SUN	
5	MON	
6	TUE	
7	WED	
8	THU	
9	FRI	
10	SAT	
11	SUN	
12	MON	
13	TUE	
14	WED	
15	THU	
16	FRI	
17	SAT	
18	SUN	
19	MON	
20	TUE	
21	WED	
22	THU	
23	FRI	
24	SAT	
25	SUN	
26	MON	
27	TUE	
28	WED	
29	THU	
30	FRI	
31	SAT	

FEBRUARY

1	SUN	
2	MON	
3	TUE	
4	WED	
5	THU	
6	FRI	
7	SAT	
8	SUN	
9	MON	
10	TUE	
11	WED	
12	THU	
13	FRI	
14	SAT	
15	SUN	
16	MON	
17	TUE	
18	WED	
19	THU	
20	FRI	
21	SAT	
22	SUN	
23	MON	
24	TUE	
25	WED	
26	THU	
27	FRI	
28	SAT	

MARCH

1	SUN	
2	MON	
3	TUE	
4	WED	
5	THU	
6	FRI	
7	SAT	
8	SUN	
9	MON	
10	TUE	
11	WED	
12	THU	
13	FRI	
14	SAT	
15	SUN	
16	MON	
17	TUE	
18	WED	
19	THU	
20	FRI	
21	SAT	
22	SUN	
23	MON	
24	TUE	
25	WED	
26	THU	
27	FRI	
28	SAT	
29	SUN	
30	MON	
31	TUE	

Be sure to share your unique approach with an accountability partner so you can inspire and learn from one another!

*An accountability partner is someone who will help you stay committed to your goals in a variety of ways.

- They can be someone who helps you stay committed to follow through on an action (think gym buddy – I need to show up for this person)
- They can be someone who motivates you to greatness (think cheer leader – my mom always says you can do anything you set your mind to)
- They can be someone who will push you to greatness (think coach – provide guidance and feedback)

The key component of an accountability partner is someone who will know if you do or do not follow through on your actions and therefore creates extra incentive for you to keep accomplishing your goals.

REFLECT AND RECORD

The power of reflecting and recording is the difference between those who wish and those who accomplish. Through the process of recording, reviewing and refining on repeat you'll be able to excel.

In multiple places throughout the GTDS Framework you'll create intention and reflection points.

In Volume 1, you will set your Quarter 1 intentions. There is an open journal-like page where you can freeform write, create a bulleted list or simply brain dump* (clear your mind by writing out your thoughts, ideas and concerns). Once it is out of your brain and on to the paper, you will feel lighter and more focused. It is also a great snapshot of what is going on in your life in that moment.

The benefits of journaling are well established. Regular reflection and brain dumping support mental clarity, emotional processing, stress reduction and personal growth.

Pro Tip: Once I have finished the quarter I find it helpful to look back and read what my intentions were before I provide my update on where the quarter ended up.

Reviewing your intentions provides a satisfying reminder of where you started and just how far you've come, leading to productive reflection.

Let's get started! 2026 here we come...

Q1 INTENTIONS

Quarter 1 Intentions

As you look ahead to planning your year, think about the quarter ahead and your ultimate BIG goals. Here are some prompts to guide your thinking:

1. **Focus Areas:** Work, family, social life, health, finances. Which areas will you prioritize this quarter?
2. **Current Status and Growth:** How do you feel mentally, physically and emotionally right now? Where and how do you want to improve over the next 90 days?
3. **Exciting Opportunities:** What upcoming events or milestones are you most excited about? How can you use that excitement to drive your progress?

At its core, the GTDS Framework is about setting intentions, recording actions, tracking progress and analyzing trends - reflecting and refining as you go. It's all about making continuous improvements one step at a time.

Start each day by confirming your top priority, scheduling your **self-care** activities and reviewing your schedule.

Whether you log your activities and accomplishments as you achieve them or at the end of your day, the important thing is to log everything!

Logging will help you on your journey to achievement. The more you record each day, the more effectively you'll be able to look back, reflect and create plans for improvement moving forward.

Before you start each week, identify the critical items you want to complete, numbers you are trying to achieve or focus items you want to address.

Pro Tip: I schedule a specific time of day, or day of the week, dedicated to my top goal to help me stay on track.

MONTH

Since humans thrive on predictability, maintaining a predictable schedule is key to your success. With a clearly defined routine, you don't need to rely on motivation or "feeling like" completing an action. You'll be able to rely on your habits to get through the challenging times.

Before you start each month, reinforce your focus and efforts by listing your Top 5 goals. Before you order your goals by priority, be sure to ask yourself if each is leading you toward your most important goal. You will reinforce the **theme of the year** each month to ensure alignment. This is your monthly score card of critical and high priority items you plan to achieve. At the end of the month, you will come back to this and be able to check off all of your accomplishments.

TOP 5 GOALS PLANNER

WORD/THEME OF THE YEAR

____

GOAL #1	ACTION STEPS
What is my goal? *Why do I want to achieve this?*	______ ______ ______ ______

GOAL #2	ACTION STEPS
What is my goal? *Why do I want to achieve this?*	______ ______ ______ ______

GOAL #3	ACTION STEPS
What is my goal? *Why do I want to achieve this?*	______ ______ ______ ______

GOAL #4	ACTION STEPS
What is my goal? *Why do I want to achieve this?*	______ ______ ______ ______

GOAL #5	ACTION STEPS
What is my goal? *Why do I want to achieve this?*	______ ______ ______ ______

Write your goal down by hand. Neuroscience confirms that writing activates different areas of the brain, strengthening focus, memory and commitment.

WEEK

Each week you will have additional opportunities to continue the important work of day-by-day updates with a running score card.

Leverage the note taking habit questions in the section above to capture insights, ideas and reflections that reinforce your learning and clarity.

The GTDS Framework will guide you in checking off the actions you complete each day. Over time, these individual actions add up, leading you to reach your goals.

Pro Tip: I've said it before and I'll say it again, always be sure to record and reflect.

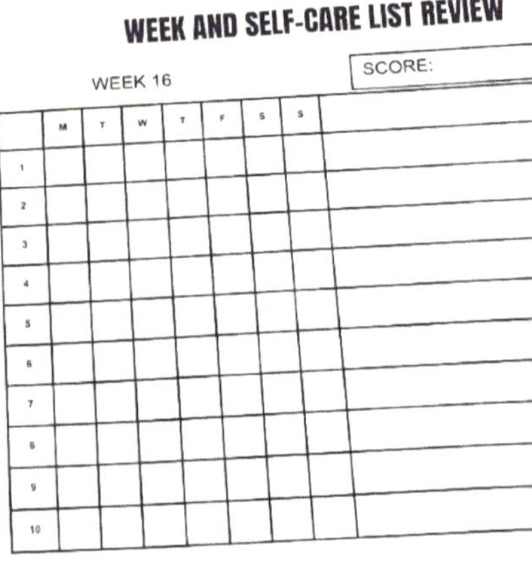

WEEK AND SELF-CARE LIST REVIEW

WEEK 1

SCORE:

	M	T	W	T	F	S	S	
1								
2								
3								
4								
5								
6								
7								
8								
9								
10								

DAY

At GTDS we believe in the importance of each and every day, so our framework provides you with ample space to record daily highlights and items to keep track of.

Pro Tip: In addition to logging my specific goal-related activities and accomplishments, I find it helpful to track other motivating items and activities like:

- Gratitude statements
- Reading material and pages read
- Favorite quotes
- Workout type and intensity
- Special events
- Important meetings
- Individual wins
- Lessons learned
- Daily **self-care** score
- Nutrition tracking
- Sleep tracking
- Emotional tracking (Even a quick doodle of a happy face, sad face, heart, etc. can be helpful.)
- Reasons to feel proud

JANUARY 2026

December 2025

Mo	Tu	We	Th	Fr	Sa	Su
1	2	3	4	5	6	7
8	9	10	11	12	13	14
15	16	17	18	19	20	21
22	23	24	25	26	27	28
29	30	31				

January

Mo	Tu	We	Th	Fr	Sa	Su
			1	2	3	4
5	6	7	8	9	10	11
12	13	14	15	16	17	18
19	20	21	22	23	24	25
26	27	28	29	30	31	

February

Mo	Tu	We	Th	Fr	Sa	Su
						1
2	3	4	5	6	7	8
9	10	11	12	13	14	15
16	17	18	19	20	21	22
23	24	25	26	27	28	

MONDAY
28

TUESDAY
29

WEDNESDAY
30

THURSDAY
1

New Year's Day

FRIDAY
2

SATURDAY
3

SUNDAY
4

WEEK 1

Mindful meditation*, even for just a few minutes a day, can help you get centered and focused. Here are some examples of positive self-talk statements and motivating mantras:

Consistently recording positive thoughts as daily highlights can help you build a strong foundation for success.

Pro Tip: I love to meditate until a positive thought pops up in my mind. When I finish meditating, I record the positive thought as one of my daily highlights. When I come back to reflect on these highlights it empowers me.

Here is what mindful meditation looks like in practice, sit somewhere quiet and comfortable for you. Consciously take a few breathes in and out and then intentionally look through your brain to find one positive word, thought, comment, etc. Stay seated until you find your positive item for the day.

Apply your Reading: Planning

- [ ] Find your accountability partner
- [ ] Complete your monthly top 5 goal planner
- [ ] Record daily actions, wins and key activities
- [ ] Conduct a weekly review to evaluate progress
- [ ] Identify one improvement for next week

Author Insight

Have you noticed I love to plan and map things out? My mother always had a To Do list in her pocket and that shaped me. Having a plan, while still staying flexible as the day unfolds, has helped me accomplish so much.

When I record consistently, I am rewarded by checking off completed items and punished by having to re-write items not completed. I am either reinforced by feeling the momentum build or motivated to cross off items from the list. Either way it helps me achieve my goals.

Once it's recorded, I review what I'm learning and adjust. If you do the same thing every day, you'll get the same results. But when you identify patterns, you can improve them.

SECTION 5

TRACK IT. REFLECT IT. EVOLVE IT.

The Power of Reflection and Growth

WEEK OVER WEEK

You can record in the weekly section by either:

1. Journaling a bit each day or on days when the mood strikes you

   OR

2. Waiting until the end of the week to journal all your weekly reflections at once

To further your reflection journey here are some great prompting questions to get you started:

- What brought you joy this week?
- What drained your energy this week?
- How did you do at accomplishing your goals and tasks?
- How are you *really* feeling?
- Did anything interesting happen this week, good or bad?

You can also spend a few minutes doing stream of consciousness writing or brain dumping.

Pro Tip: If I did NOT accomplish a **self-care** action on more than four days in one week, I find it helpful to highlight it in red. What contingencies did I overlook and how can I correct them?

Tracking items you didn't accomplish makes it easy to flip through pages and quickly get a visual representation of your opportunity areas for improvement. It also provides useful insight into trends at the end of the week, month, quarter and year.

WEEK AND SELF-CARE LIST REVIEW

WEEK 1

SCORE:

	M	T	W	T	F	S	S	
1								
2								
3								
4								
5								
6								
7								
8								
9								
10								

Time Awareness Exercise: Track Your Day

Before you can improve how you spend your time, you need to understand where your time is currently going.

This simple exercise will help you build awareness, identify patterns and make more intentional choices with your time.

Step 1: Track Your Day (One Full Day Minimum but we recommend at least a week as different days will have variations in typical schedules.)

For one full day, write down what you are doing throughout the day.

- Track in 30-60 minute blocks
- Be honest, this is for your awareness, not judgment
- Include everything (work, breaks, scrolling, conversations, etc.)

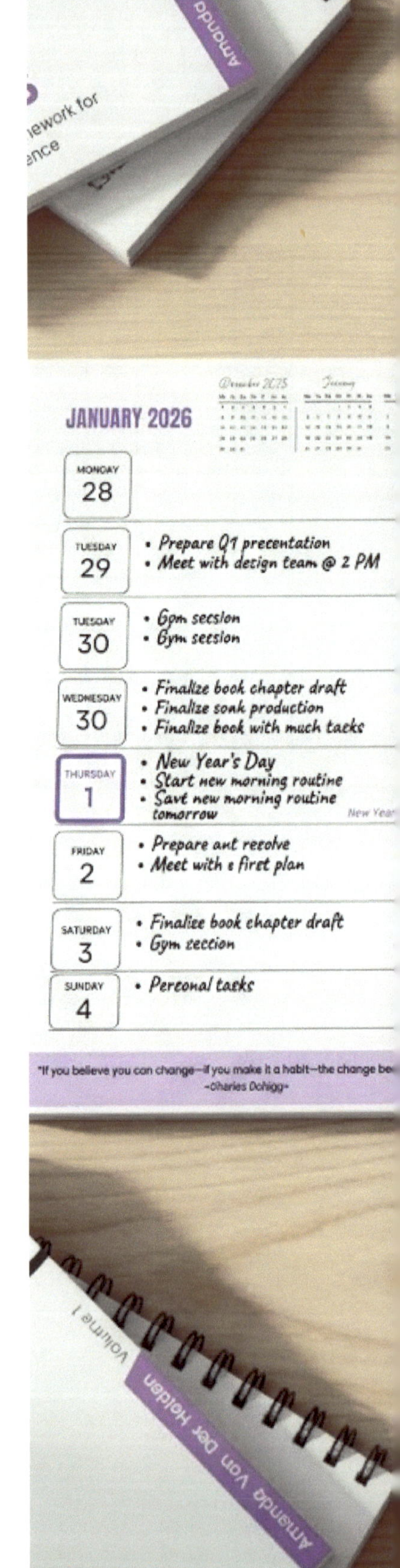

Time	Activity	Actual
5-6 am	Wake up, work out, meditate and learn something	45 min
6-7 am	Feed the horses and clean the barn	30 min
7-8 am	Get the kids ready and off to school	80 min
8-10 am	Meetings	180 min
1-3 pm	GTDS Authorized Consultant Program Foundation course	30 min
3-3:30 pm	Emails	40 min
3:30-4 pm	Kids post-school routine	45 min
4-5 pm	Feed the horses and clean the barn	40 min
5-6 pm	Wrap up work items and prepare for tomorrow's meetings	50 min
6-8 pm	Evening routine + Family Time	90 min
8-9 pm	Self-care	60 min
9 pm	Sleep	8 hrs

The more specific you can be here the more you will really be able to add up where all your minutes went this week.

Step 2: Identify Patterns

At the end of the day, review your entries and reflect:

- Where did my time go today?
- What activities created the most value?
- Where did I lose time or get distracted?
- When was my energy highest and lowest?

Step 3: Categorize Your Time

Label each activity:

- High Value (moves you toward your goals)
- Necessary (required but not goal-driving)
- Low Value (distractions, time leaks)

Step 4: Make One Adjustment

Start small and always make one change at a time to see the impact of that change.

Ask yourself:

What is one thing I can do differently tomorrow?

Examples:

- Block time for focused work
- Reduce distractions during a key hour
- Start the day with a priority task

Pro Tip: One of my favorite quotes is "What gets measured gets managed" - Peter Drucker

MONTH OVER MONTH

Buckle up, there's a lot to cover when it comes to reviewing your month and recording your reflections. Each month provides a built-in opportunity for you to provide high level updates.

If you follow the GTDS Framework by journaling daily and weekly, at the end of the month your first step will be to read through your journal entries and track what you recorded.

Now that you have completed the track your time exercise, be sure to keep tracking. By continuing to log where your time is being spent (in real-time as much as possible) you will be able to clearly see where you are investing the time that makes up your life.

Top 10 Items I spent my time on

☐ **# of perfect days**

1		6	
2		7	
3		8	
4		9	
5		10	

At the end of the month you will be able to easily identify the top ten activity areas your time was spent that month. This information will help you make tweaks to use your time more effectively in the month ahead. This is why the monthly review and monthly intention sections are placed next to each other.

Quick example, let's say you watch one episode of TV each night. For that day and in that moment, it doesn't seem like that much time. It may only be 30-60minutes a day, but over the course of the month you realize that accounted for 31 hours and it is in your top 10 time slots. You may decide that 30+ hours could be focused on spending more quality time with your family or something else that would give you joy and energize you.

In addition to the above, you'll also want to look back at:

- Your calendar, meetings and phone logs of who you spent time with
- Pictures you took that may trigger ideas and memories
- Financial records that show where you're spending your money

Pro Tip: As I read through past entries from the month, I like to use a piece of scrap paper to write down a list of themes, key events, topics or whatever strikes me. Afterwards, I work that list into my reflection and journaling time.

Reflection without action or adjustment is less likely to impact change or improvement. Journaling for the sake of journaling is great and offers the psychological benefits of getting the thoughts out of your head and onto paper. But the real magic comes from gaining those benefits in addition to understanding yourself deeper by reflecting on trends, themes and overall thought patterns. Once you've combined these actions, it becomes clear to see what's needed to set yourself up for success in the future!

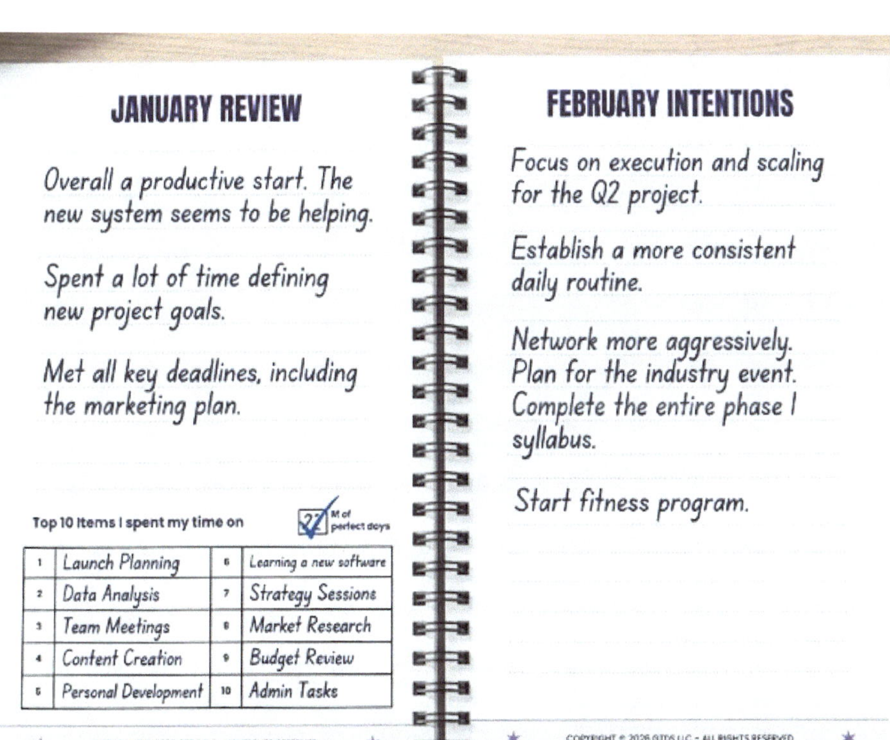

Here are some additional reflection questions to get you started:

- What were the overall trends or themes you noticed this month?
- Are you on track with your goals? Why or why not?
- What am I most proud of?
- What was the most disappointing part of this month?
- The BEST thing that happened was....

Pro Tip: I like to use the month calendar to record ONE accomplishment on each day. Since there isn't a lot of space on the calendar, I'm forced to choose only the most important item. This makes it easy to review a month of daily focal points.

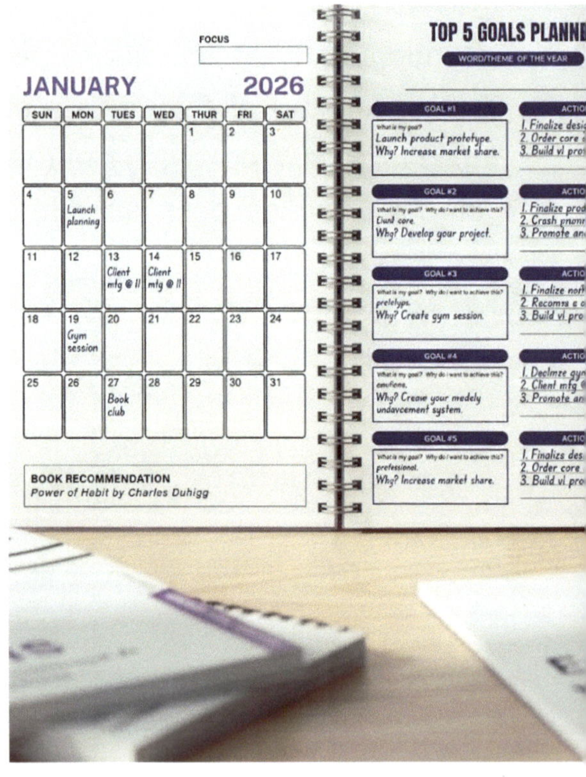

FOCUS

JANUARY 2026

SUN	MON	TUES	WED	THUR	FRI	SAT
				1	2	3
4	5	6	7	8	9	10
11	12	13	14	15	16	17
18	19	20	21	22	23	24
25	26	27	28	29	30	31

BOOK RECOMMENDATION
Power of Habit by Charles Duhigg

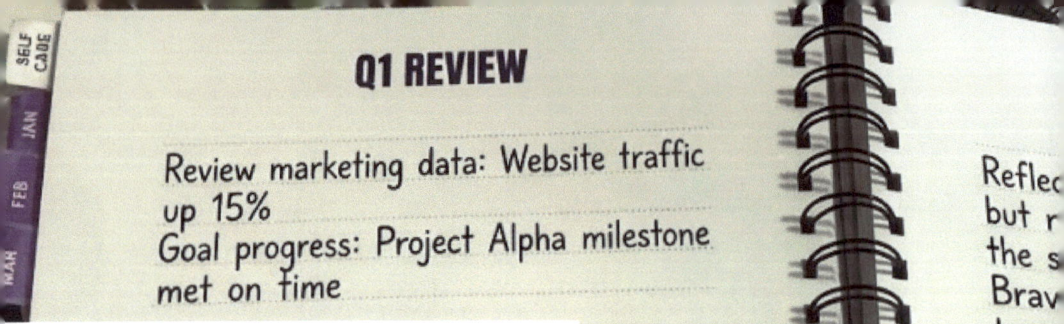

QUARTER OVER QUARTER

At the end of three months, there is a quarterly review. Just like days and weeks build up to a month, when reviewing for the quarter I typically re-review the monthly logs, goals and scores.

In addition to reviewing, the quarterly reflection is a critical point for looking at how you are tracking against your annual goal. Are you on schedule or behind? What will it take to accomplish what you set out to achieve?

Additional quarter reflection questions:

- What actions created the greatest impact?
- What challenges did I face and what did I learn?
- How did I show up in my relationships and communication?
- What fueled me?

Q1 REVIEW

Just like the months that came before, it's always useful to look back at the intentions and goals you set out at the beginning to see what you accomplished, what targets you missed and record what you plan to change in the future.

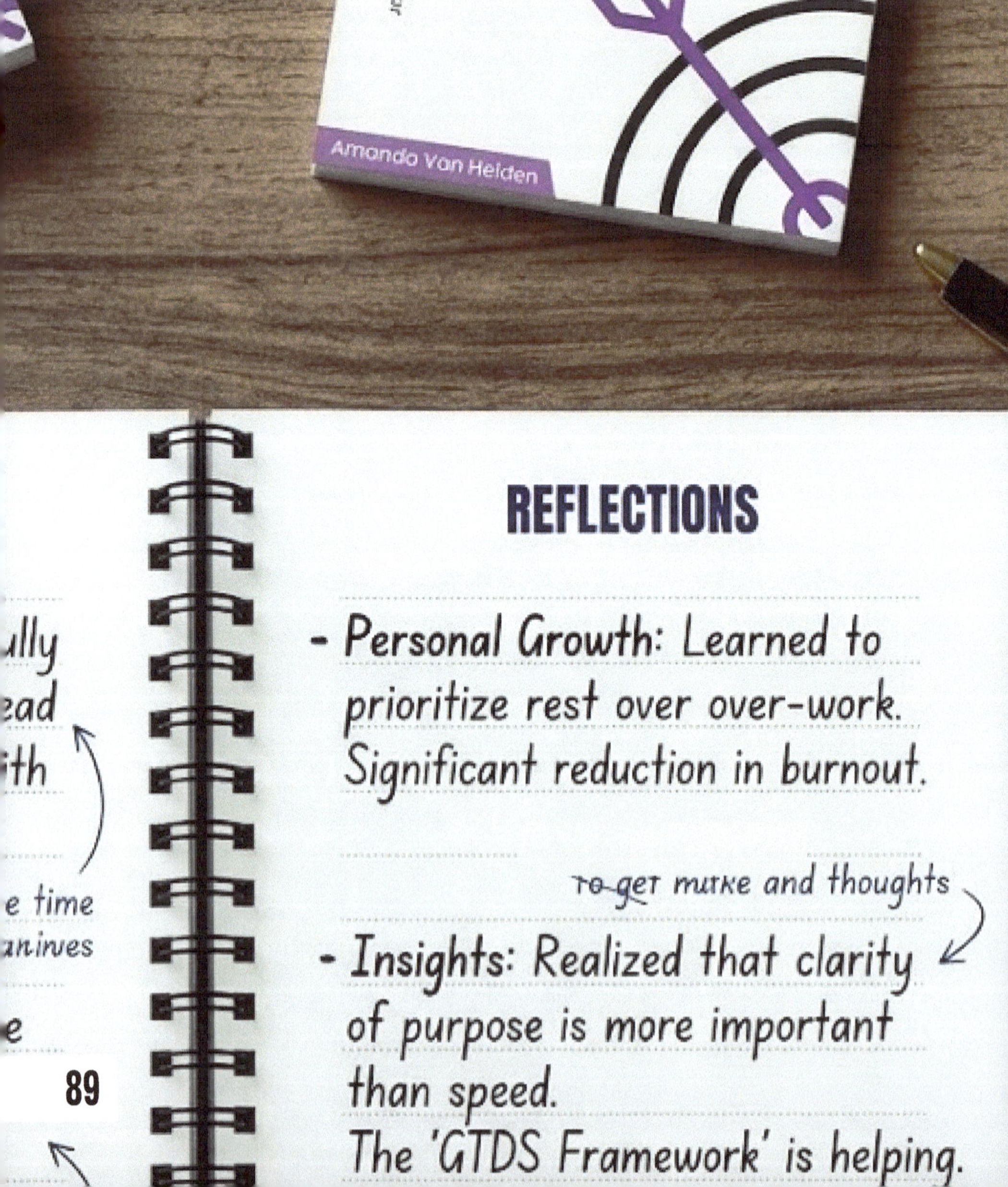

REFLECTIONS

MID-YEAR

After living through half of your year, what do you have to show for it? To find out, go back and review your Q1 and Q2 intentions, reflections, progress, trends and everything else. Are you sensing a pattern? Each reflection and intention page will build on the other to move you forward.

As with any project, a critical component is understanding where you are at in the plan, identifying any risks to achieving the goal and most importantly adjusting your plan to ensure success.

The same is true for the halfway point in the year: it's a critical time to track how much progress has been made towards your goals and then identify how much further you have to go to achieve them.

Here are some additional mid-year reflection questions:

- What is the biggest trend for the last six months?
- What unexpected win or moment surprised me the most?
- What habit or action has made the biggest difference so far?
- What has been derailing me and how can I minimize it for the rest of the year?
- Where have I shown up with more intention or where do I want to?
- How have I been using my **Word or Theme of the Year**?

MID YEAR REVIEW

END OF YEAR

When the year comes to an end, congratulate yourself! You lived another year on this earth and it's time to review and reflect on all that transpired. You'll notice this section has the most space for you to take all that you have learned and reflect. The highs and lows, the wins and losses all add up to something; now it's time to determine just what that is.

As the year ends, these reflection questions will help guide you forward:

- In the future, when I look back at this year, what do I want to remember from this year? Why?
- What did I try this year that took courage?
- What has this year taught me about how I work best?
- What skill, mindset or behavior have I improved the most?
- When things went wrong this year, how well did I recover? Did I think of it negatively as a failure or positively as an opportunity to learn?
- In the future, when I look back at this year, what do I want to remember from this year? Why?
- What did I try this year that took courage?
- What has this year taught me about how I work best?
- What skill, mindset or behavior have I improved the most?

- How did I grow this year:
    - Personally?
    - Professionally?
    - In my relationships? Who had the biggest positive impact on me this year? Who had the most negative impact? How did I show up for the people in my life and show them I cared?
- Which goals did I achieve or make progress toward?
- Which goals evolved or changed and what did I learn?
- What mattered most to me this year, based on how I spent my time?
- How well did I care for myself while pursuing my goals?
- Compared to the start of the year, what does "success" look like to me now?

After all of your hard work methodically tracking your time, energy, **self-care, word/theme**, journal, quotes, pictures, activities and so much more—your win/joy/accomplishment jar* gives you a chance to reminisce about the best moments, a perfect ending to a long year!

Pro Tip: Throughout the year I like to keep a win/joy/accomplishment jar where I keep reminders of moments, big and small, that filled me with happiness.

Apply your Reading: Reflection and Growth

- [ ] Complete Your Time Awareness Exercise
- [ ] Answer reflection questions
- [ ] Start a win/joy/accomplishment jar
- [ ] Log 10 items you spent the most time on this month
- [ ] Complete your reflection and intention sections
- [ ] Identify one pattern: What energized you and what drained you?

Author Insight

For years, I spent time being busy. Running around and doing, but not feeling productive.

When I started logging my days, patterns quickly emerged. I could clearly see where I was making progress and where I was losing time. That awareness changed everything.

Instead of guessing, I could make intentional adjustments. I didn't try to change everything all at once, I focused on one small improvement at a time.

Over time, intentionally designing my days and choosing my habits resulted in meaningful impact.

SECTION 6

CONNECT IT. CELEBRATE IT. CONTINUE IT.

The Power of Continuous Improvement

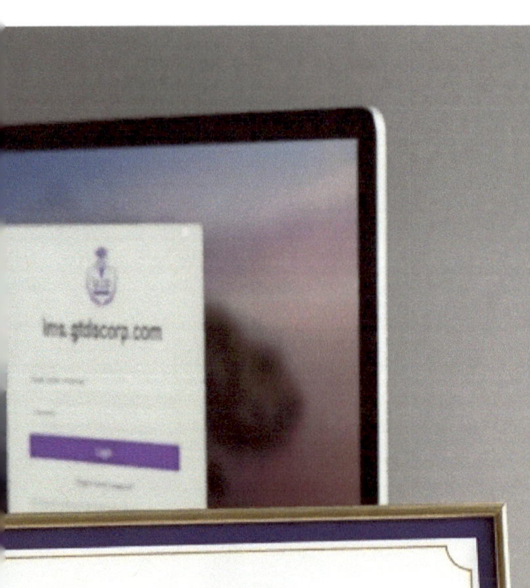
lms.gtdscorp.com

GTDS

CERTIFICATE
of Completion
This is to certify that
Amanda Van Der Heiden
has successfully finished the necessary course of study and met all test criteria for the GTDS Authorized Consultant Credential, along with all associated rights and privileges.
March 16, 2026

Amanda Van Der Heiden
COO, GTDS LLC.

Excel
with
Your
Goals
The GTDS Framework for
Personal Excellence
Amanda Van Der Heiden
Volume I

GTDS

Set
Yourself
Up to
Excel
GTDS
A Practical Guide to
Goals, Habits, and Success
Amanda Van Der Heiden

CLOSING REMARKS

I'm so excited for you to begin this journey of continuous improvement to build the best version of yourself... strategically, intentionally and with great ambition.

As you look back, I hope you're proud of how far you've come and excited for what's ahead.

Remember that these activities and questions are great, but they're useless unless you **DO** them. Be sure to go through each activity and really give it your all. Your future self will thank you!

I would love to hear from you. If you have questions or simply want to share how you've used the GTDS Framework, please reach out. I look forward to hearing what you accomplish and where you plan to go next.

Thank you for committing your time and energy to the GTDS Framework.

If you are interested in gaining all the benefits of the GTDS Framework for Excellence, check out the full program that builds on these techniques here: https://lms.gtdscorp.com/

PARTNERSHIPS THAT EMPOWER,
SOLUTIONS THAT DRIVE IMPACT.

BONUS CONTENT

If you still want more, here's a bonus system to use within the larger system I created.

I've mentioned there are many ways the Quarter Planner section can be leveraged, including using it like a score card.

This section is optional but since many people have asked about it, I'm sharing how it can provide a visual snapshot of your year. Take what you like and leave what you don't.

Using the Quarter Planner, I track a few critical metrics:

- **Self-care** score at the beginning and end of the month
- Weight at the beginning and end of each month and one final on the last day of the year
- Nutrition achievements
- Workout achievements
- Step count achievements
- Sleep goal achievements
- Travel completed

To make it easy to quickly track items and trends, I color-code my planner using a multi-colored pen (or different colored pens).

As you can see from this example, the result looks like a score card:

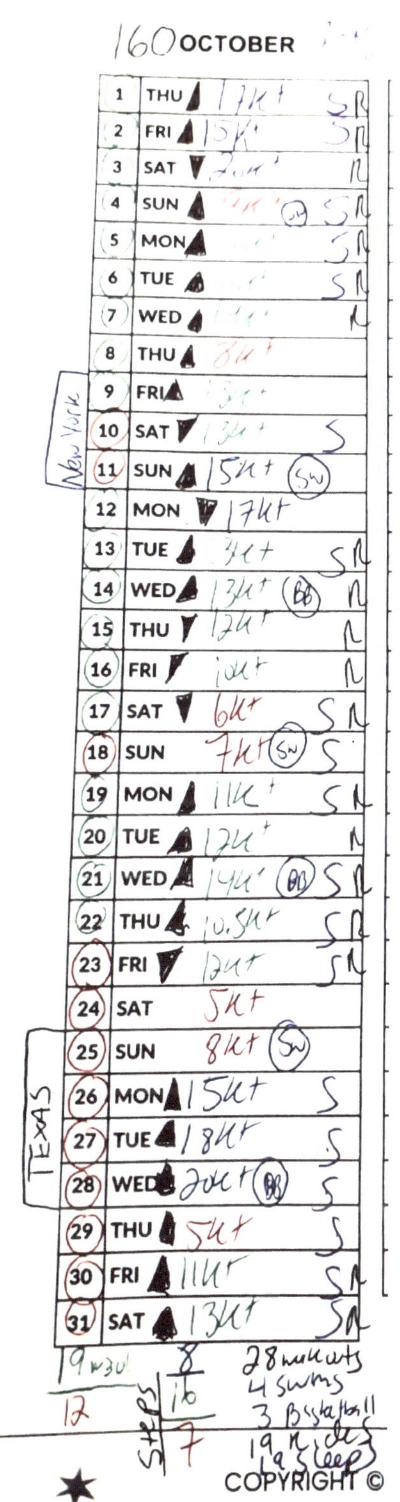

Pro Tip: Make It Visual

Use colors to quickly see patterns and trends. You can instantly spot what's working and what needs attention.

RECOMMENDED READING

For optimal results, continue moving forward with the GTDS Framework:

- **Volume 1: Excel With Your Goals:** The GTDS Framework for Excellence by Amanda Van Der Heiden - This is the workbook thoughtfully put together for you leveraging all the framework and activities described in this book. The focus is on how you lead yourself and accomplish your goals by creating strong habits and infusing motivation along the way.

Here are additional books that can help you as you work toward achieving your goals:

- **The Whole30: The 30-Day Guide to Total Health and Food Freedom** by Melissa Hartwig Urban
- **The Power of Habit: Why We Do What We Do in Life and Business** by Charles Duhigg
- **Atomic Habits: An Easy & Proven Way to Build Good Habits & Break Bad Ones** by James Clear
- **The 7 Habits of Highly Effective People: Powerful Lessons in Personal Change** by Stephen R. Covey
- **The One Thing: The Surprisingly Simple Truth Behind Extraordinary Results** by Gary W. Keller and Jay Papasan
- **Mindset: The New Psychology of Success** by Carol S. Dweck
- **Grit: The Power of Passion and Perseverance** by Angela Duckworth
- **Attitude is Everything: Change Your Attitude... Change Your Life!** by Jeff Keller
- **The 5 AM Club** by Robin Sharma
- **Make Your Bed: Little Things That Can Change Your Life...And Maybe the World** by William H. McRaven
- **Start with Why: How Great Leaders Inspire Everyone to Take Action** by Simon Sinek
- **Emotional Intelligence: Why It Can Matter More Than IQ** by Daniel Goleman
- **Bluefishing: The Art of Making Things Happen** by Steve Sims

FUTURE RECOMMENDATIONS

Continue your journey with the GTDS Framework series:

- **Volume 2: Excel with Your People (2027)**
  - The next annual workbook in the series builds upon the foundation of Volume 1 and focuses on how to build and maintain strong relationships.
- **Volume 3: Excel in Your Organization (2028)**
  - The next annual workbook in the series continues the framework for excellence by building on what you have learned about leading yourself and working with others and now focuses on how you can succeed with teams and organizations.
- **Volume 4: Excel with Your Change (2029)**
  - The next annual workbook in the series, provides you with the tools for you to succeed during times of change.
- **Volume 5: The Excel series continues in 2030**

RECOMMENDED TOOLS

The GTDS team loves using these tools and tech along with our framework:

- 7 Minute Workout app (Fitness)
- Toggl app (Time tracking)
- Fitbit (Wellness)
- Apple Watch (Time tracking and wellness)

Pro Tip: Simplify Your Tools

Ultimately, the best tool is the one you actually use consistently. Start with ONE tool at a time, build the habit of using it daily and enhance your overall system before moving on to the next tool.

Terms and Definitions

Here is a quick reference guide to words, terms and phrases introduced in the book and their definitions.

Accountability Partner: A person who supports your goals by providing encouragement, check-ins and shared commitment to follow-through.

Analysis Paralysis: A state of overthinking or overanalyzing that prevents decision-making or action.

Anticipatory Anxiety: Stress or worry about a future event, often based on imagined outcomes rather than reality.

Brain Dump: A technique where you write down all thoughts, tasks or concerns to clear mental clutter and improve focus.

Cognitive Dissonance: The mental discomfort experienced when actions, beliefs or values are inconsistent with one another.

Confirmation Bias: The tendency to seek out or interpret information in a way that confirms existing beliefs.

Contingency Plans: Pre-planned responses or backup strategies to address potential obstacles or challenges.

Extrinsically Motivated: Driven by external rewards or pressures, such as recognition, money or expectations.

Frequency Illusion: Also known as the Baader-Meinhof phenomenon; when something you've recently noticed suddenly appears more frequently.

Gamifying: Applying game-like elements (points, challenges, rewards) to tasks to increase motivation and engagement.

Intention Offloading: Using external cues (like post-it notes, images or calendars) to reduce the amount of items you need to remember in your brain and instead leverage other ways to create a daily prompt for action.

Intrinsically Motivated: Driven by internal satisfaction, enjoyment, purpose or personal meaning.

Micro-Challenge: A small, manageable task designed to build momentum and confidence toward a larger goal.

Mindful Meditation: A practice of focusing attention on the present moment with awareness and intention.

Neuroscience: The study of the brain and nervous system, including how thoughts, behaviors and emotions are processed.

Note-Taking Habit: The practice of consistently capturing insights, ideas and reflections to reinforce learning and clarity.

Personal Playbook: A collection of notes, lessons, strategies and reminders that guide your actions and decision-making.

Reverse Engineer: A goal-setting approach that starts with the desired outcome and works backward to identify the steps needed to achieve it.

Selective Attention: The ability to focus on specific information while filtering out distractions.

Self-Care: Intentional actions taken to support physical, mental, emotional and social well-being.

Self-Efficacy: The belief in your ability to successfully complete tasks and achieve goals.

SMARTER Goals: A goal-setting framework: Specific, Measurable, Achievable, Relevant/Realistic, Timely, Evaluate and Refine.

Time Blocking: A scheduling method where time is allocated in advance for specific tasks or activities.

Visualization Techniques: The practice of mentally imagining desired outcomes to increase motivation and likelihood of success.

Vision Cover: A personalized visual representation of your goals, intentions and desired future used for daily inspiration.

Weak Ties: Connections outside your close circle (acquaintances or friends of friends) that often provide new opportunities, perspectives and information.

Whole30: A 30-day nutritional program focused on whole, unprocessed foods to reset eating habits and improve awareness of food choices.

Win / Joy / Accomplishment Jar: A collection of written moments of success, gratitude or achievement to reflect on progress and build positivity.

Word or Theme of the Year: A guiding word or concept chosen to focus intentions, decisions and actions throughout the year.

Pro Tip: Create your own glossary of words you learn and love.

Apply your Reading: Reflection and Growth

- [ ] Create your own color-coded scorecard system
- [ ] Choose your next book to read
- [ ] Build your personal glossary of key terms
- [ ] Purchase Volume 1 to continue your journey

Author Insight

I've learned so much from living, building and applying this framework over the past decade!

Now it is your turn.

The more energy and intention you put into the exercises, questions and processes in this book, the more progress you will achieve. Remember that big change happens one small, intentional, action step at a time followed by another and another and another. You need to consistently push forward, keep learning and keep growing. You can do anything you set your mind to.

Go make it happen...

GTDS Activity Index

A Complete Guide to Applying the GTDS Framework

How to Use This Index

- Revisit exercises when you feel stuck
- Focus on one category at a time
- Repeat key activities to deepen results
- Track your consistency to see your results

Use this index as a quick reference to revisit exercises, reinforce key concepts and continue building momentum throughout your journey.

Mindset & Awareness

- [ ] Practice Positive Visualization
- [ ] Remove Distractions
- [ ] Practice Mindful Meditation
- [ ] Identify Your Energy Sources
- [ ] Align Your Identity & Goals

Goal Development

- [ ] Five Whys Exercise
- [ ] Set SMARTER Goals
- [ ] Reverse Engineer Your Goals
- [ ] Prioritize Your Goals
- [ ] Create Contingency Plans
- [ ] Accomplish Your Goals

Action & Execution

- [ ] Create a Micro-Challenge
- [ ] Time Blocking Exercise
- [ ] Identify Your Next Action
- [ ] Design Your Ideal Day
- [ ] Find Your Accountability Partner

Planning & Systems

- [ ] Set up Your Planner System
- [ ] Develop Note-Taking Habit
- [ ] Build Your Personal Playbook
- [ ] Create Color-Coded Scorecard
- [ ] Complete Your Top 5

Tracking & Measurement

- [ ] Tracking & Measuring Exercise
- [ ] Time Awareness Exercise
- [ ] Record Daily Actions
- [ ] One Priority Per Day

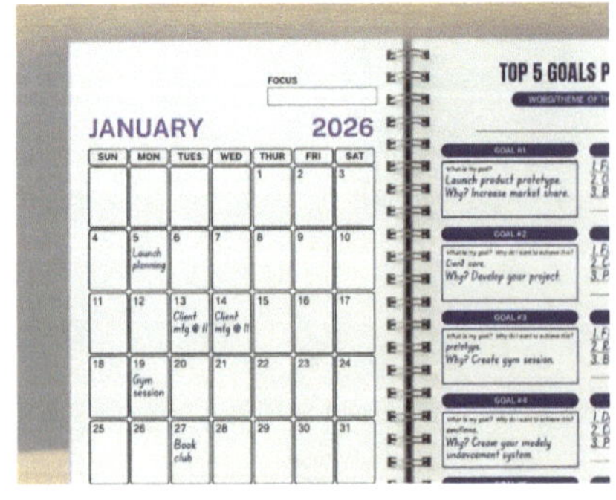

Reflection & Growth

- [ ] Journal and Reflect Exercises
- [ ] Weekly Reflection and Adjustment
- [ ] Monthly Review and Insights
- [ ] Quarterly Reflection
- [ ] Mid-Year Reflection
- [ ] End-of-Year Reflection
- [ ] 3-Step Reset Exercise
- [ ] Apply the GTDS 3-R Method (Record – Review – Refine)

Lifestyle & Identity Design

- [ ] Create your Self-Care List
- [ ] Select Your Word/Theme
- [ ] Bring Your Word to Life
- [ ] Create Your Vision Cover

Continuous Improvement & Expansion

- [ ] Review Progress & Patterns
- [ ] Build Personal Glossary
- [ ] Choose Your Next Book
- [ ] Create a Win Jar
- [ ] ***Continue with Volume 1 of the GTDS Framework***

GTDS Introduction

For more than 20 years, GTDS has helped organizations achieve measurable business outcomes by aligning people, processes, systems, tools and training. We partner with leaders to solve complex challenges, accelerate execution and deliver results that last. Using the GTDS Framework for Excellence, our certified Consultants bring the right expertise at the right time, whether you need short-term support or a long-term transformation partner.

We have provided services for more than 50 industry leading companies world-wide.

People	**100+**
Countries	**15+**
Languages	**10+**
Clients	**50+**
Industries	**12+**
Years	**20+**

GTDS Pillars of Service

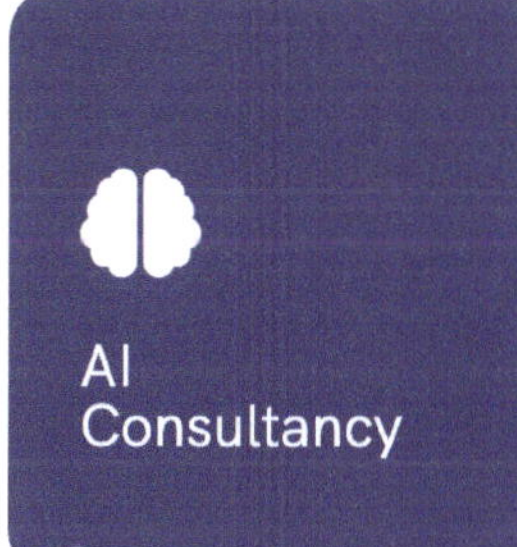

Special Bonuses

You're serious about your growth and we want to help. Schedule your **FREE Goal Setting** call today.

As a reader of this book, you can also access the GTDS proprietary **Template Giveaway** which is used across our Fortune 500 Clients!

Global Talent Development Solutions

Global Talent Development Solutions LLC
www.GTDScorp.com
contact@gtdscorp.com
ISBN: **979-8-9942006-2-9**

www.ingramcontent.com/pod-product-compliance
Lightning Source LLC
LaVergne TN
LVHW052253100826
845147LV00001B/31

* 9 7 9 8 9 9 4 2 0 0 6 2 9 *